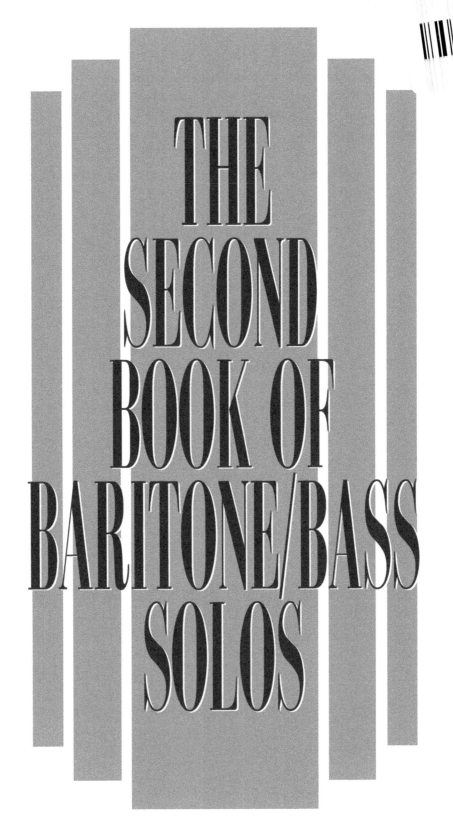

THE SECOND BOOK OF BARITONE/BASS SOLOS

compiled by Joan Frey Boytim

G. SCHIRMER, Inc.

DISTRIBUTED BY

HAL•LEONARD®
CORPORATION

7777 W. BLUEMOUND RD. P.O. BOX 13819 MILWAUKEE, WI 53213

PREFACE

The eight volumes that comprise "The First Book of Solos" and "The First Book of Solos—Part II" were compiled to provide a great variety of song literature at the same basic level of difficulty for students at the beginning stages of voice study. The four volumes in "The Second Book of Solos" are designed to contribute to musical and vocal development at the next progressive level of study.

The majority of these songs require more vocal sophistication than those found in the earlier volumes. Singers using this set will be exposed to songs with wider ranges that require more vocal flexibility and vocal control, and that make greater use of the dramatic qualities of the voice. The student who can sing many of the songs in the "The First Book" and "The First Book—Part II" will be ready for the challenges found in "The Second Book of Solos."

The general format of songs remains the same as the previous collections, with a representative group of songs in English, Italian, German, and French from various periods of music history, as well as selected sacred solos. Added are several songs from Gilbert and Sullivan operettas and solos from the oratorio repertoire. Numerous pieces previously available only in single sheet form and many songs that for some time have been out of print are included.

I want to thank Richard Walters for encouraging the development of this practical song literature series. The twelve books, taken together, provide a comprehensive, inexpensive collection of 400 songs for the voice teacher and student.

Joan Frey Boytim

About the Compiler...

Since 1968, Joan Frey Boytim has owned and operated a full-time voice studio in Carlisle, Pennsylvania, where she has specialized in developing a serious and comprehensive curriculum and approach to teaching and coaching adolescent and community adult students. Her teaching experience has also included music and choral instruction at the junior high and senior high levels, and voice instruction at the college level. She is the author of the widely used bibliography, *Solo Vocal Repertoire for Young Singers* (a publication of NATS), and, as a nationally recognized expert on teaching beginning vocal study, is a frequent speaker and clinician on the topic.

CONTENTS

AH! WILLOW

arranged by H. Lane Wilson

To the brook and the wil - low_ that_ heard him com -
- plain, Ah! wil - low, wil - low! Poor Col - in went_

weep - ing and told them his _____ pain; Ah!

wil - low, wil - - - low! Ah!__ wil - low, wil - low!

"Dear

stream, if you chance by__ her__ pil - - low to creep, Ah!

I WILL SING NEW SONGS

from Biblical Songs

Antonín Dvořák

I will sing new songs of glad-ness, I will sing Je -

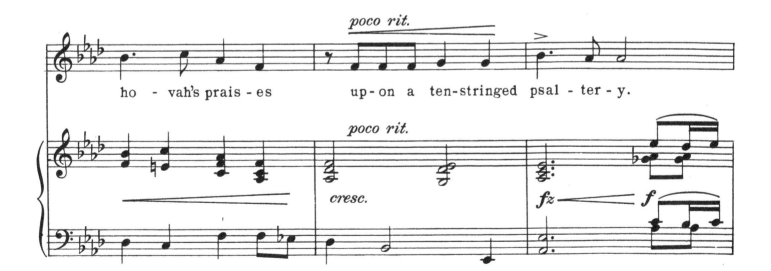

ho - vah's prais - es up-on a ten-stringed psal - ter-y.

Ev - 'ry day will I ex - tol Thee and will bless Thy

Ho - ly Name, I will bless Thy Ho - ly Name.

Great is God and great His mer-cy. Who shall tell of

all His great-ness? Who shall His pow'r de-clare?

My song__ shall be of

praise and hon - or, and of Thy glo - rious acts. Thy

works are won - der - ful, past our

know-ing. Yea, men shall tell of Thy great kind - ness and

of Thy won-d'rous might, and my voice shall pro-

claim a-loud Thy glo-ry.

ANNIE LAURIE

Words by William Douglas
Revised and third verse added by Lady John Scott

Melody by Lady John Scott
Accompaniment by
J.B. Wekerlin

13

me her prom - ise true.
e'er the sun shone on.

(Gie'd)
Gave me her prom - ise
That e'er the sun shone

(Which ne'er for - got will

And ne'er for - get will
And dark blue is her

true,
on,

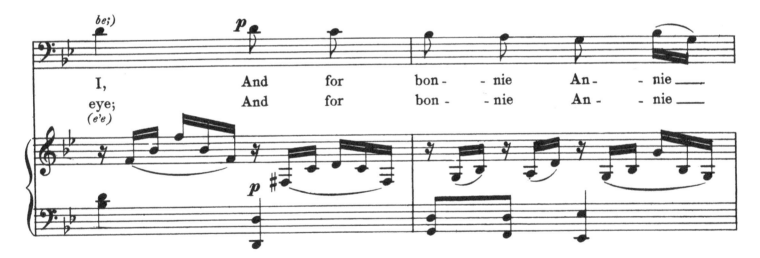

be;)
(e'e)

I,
eye;

And for bon - nie An - nie
And for bon - nie An - nie

Lau - rie I'd lay me down and die.
Lau - rie I'd lay me down and die.

(doon) *(dee)*
(doon) *(dee)*

suivez *a tempo*

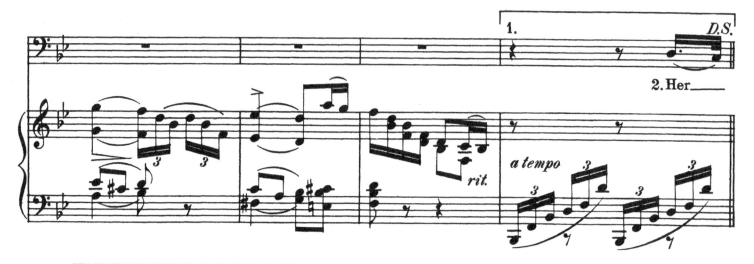

1. D.S.

2. Her____

2. *p*

3. Like__ dew on the gow - -an ly - ing, Is the

fall of her dain- -ty__ feet; _____ And like
(fa')

poco rit.

winds in sum- -mer sigh - ing, Her voice is__ low and

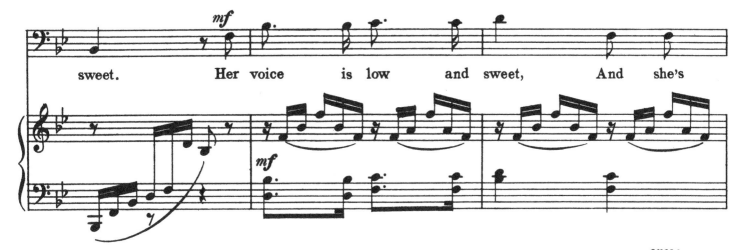

sweet. Her voice is low and sweet, And she's

a' the world to me; And for

bon - -nie An - nie Lau - rie I'd

lay me down and die.
(doon) (dee)

ARISE, YE SUBTERRANEAN WINDS

From "The Tempest"

Henry Purcell

Quickly

A-rise, a-rise, ye sub -

- - - - - - ter - ra - nean winds,

stacc.

winds, More to dis - tract their guilt - y minds!

p

A - rise, ___ ye winds, a - rise, ___ ye

winds, whose rap - - - - - id _ force can

make All but the fix'd, all,

all but the fix'd _____ and

sol - - - - - id cen - tre shake.

Come drive these

wretches to __ that __ part o'th'Isle, Where Na - ture nev - er, where

Na - ture nev - er, nev - er __ yet did smile:

Cause fogs and

damps, whirl - - winds and earth-quakes there, There let them

howl _____ and lan - - guish, lan -

- - guish in de - spair! Rise __ and o - bey!

Rise — and o - bey! Rise — and o - bey —

the pow'r - - - - - - - -

- - - - - - - - -

- ful Prince, the — pow'r - - ful Prince o' th'air!

rall.

colla voce

ARM, ARM, YE BRAVE

from Judas Maccabaeus

George Frideric Handel

ear; and points out Mac-ca-bae-us to their aid. Ju-das shall set the cap-tive

free, And lead us on to vic-to-ry!

Allegro.

Arm, arm ye brave!

24

In de - fence of your na - tion, re - li - gion, and laws, Th'al -

might - y Je - ho - vah will strength - en your hands; In de -

fence of your na - tion, re - li - gion, and laws,

Th'al - might - y Je - ho - vah will strength - - - - -

LE CHARME

Armand Silvestre
English version by Henry G. Chapman

Ernest Chausson

Mais ce que se-rait cet é--moi, Je ne pus d'a-bord en ré-
What this sud-den pas-sion might be, 'Twas be-yond my pow'r to de-

pon - dre. Ce qui me vain - quit à ja - mais, Ce
fine me. But the charm that made me your slave Is

fut un plus dou-lou-reux char-me; Et je n'ai su que je t'ai-
one that grief holds in its keep-ing: I did not know 'twas love I

mais, Qu'en voy - ant ta pre-miè - re lar - me.
gave, Till that day when I found you weep - ing.

CHILD OF THE FLOWING TIDE

Geoffrey Dearmer

Martin Shaw

Printed in the U.S.A. by G. Schirmer, Inc.

two of them saddled for you and for me, Are pawing and stamping the

surf to be free Where the wild sea - hors - es ride,

The deep wa - ters shall roar as we

race from the shore On the back of the flow - ing

tide._____

O

hur-ry, the moon is a-way in the sky (Child of the flow-ing

tide) With your heels well down, and your heart set high You're

saddled and bri-dled, and so am I; So gath-er your reins, for the

foam will fly Where the wild sea - hors-es ride,_____ Grip

tight with your knees_ as you gal - lop the seas. On the

back_ of the flow - - ing_ tide._____

On the

wide la - goon I'll meet you to - night (Child of the flow - ing

tide) When the moon swings high and the stars are a - light

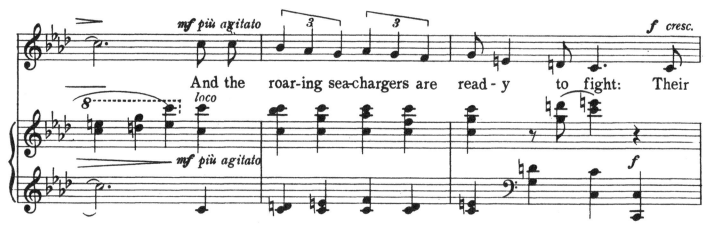

And the roar-ing sea-chargers are read - y to fight: Their

manes are all foam and their coats all white Where the wild sea - hors - es

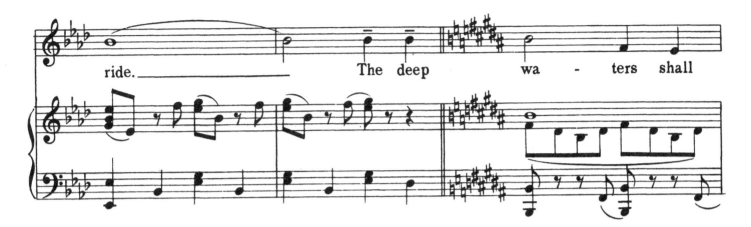

ride._____ The deep wa - ters shall

roar___ as we race_ to the shore On the

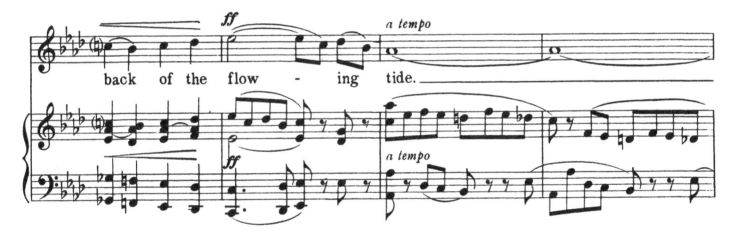

back of the flow - ing tide._____

COME, YE BLESSED

Matthew xxv : 34 - 36

John Prindle Scott

from the foun-da-tion of __ the world, from the foun-da - tion

of the world. Come, ye bless-ed of __ my Fa - ther, in-

her - it the king-dom pre - pared for you _____ from the foun-da - tion

of the world. Come, ye bless-ed of __ my Fa-ther. _____

Poco più mosso

I was an - hun - gered, and __ ye gave me meat;

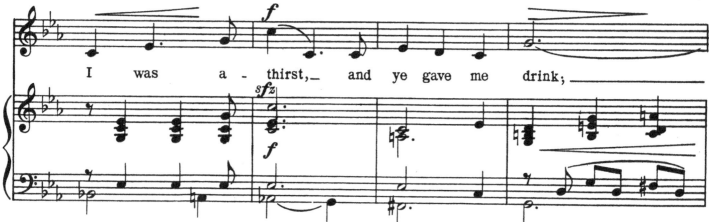

I was a - thirst, __ and ye gave me drink; _____

I was a stran - ger, and ye took me

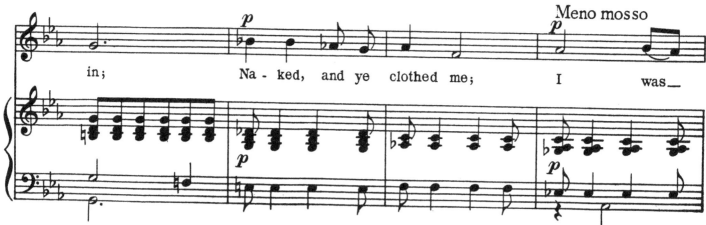

in; Na - ked, and ye clothed me; I was __

sick,   sick,   and ye vis - it - ed   me;

I   was in pris - on, and ye   came un - to   me,   ye

f largamente

rit. e dim.

came un - to   me. _____

a tempo

rit.   ***p** rit.*   *without breathing*

There - fore,

Tempo I°

come,___ ye bless - ed of my Fa - ther, in -

her - it the king - dom pre - pared ___ for you

from the foun - da - tion of___ the world, in - her - it the king-dom pre-pared for

you from the foun - da - tion of the world.

Come,__ ye bless - ed of_____ my Fa - ther,

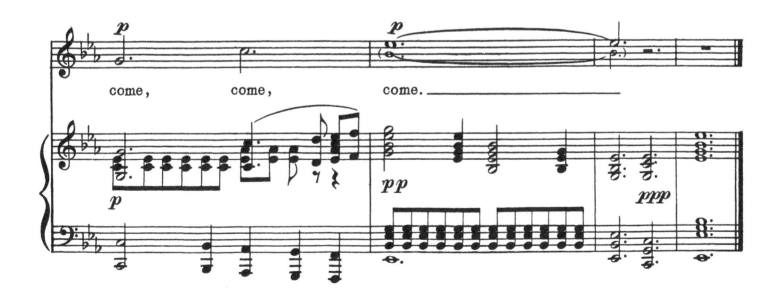

come, come, come._____

GEFROR'NE THRÄNEN

from Die Winterreise
by Wilhelm Müller
Translation by Theodore Baker

(Frozen Tears)

Franz Schubert

Some froz-en teardrops creeping A-down my cheek do flow; Have I been really
Ge - fror'-ne Tropfen fal - len von mei-nen Wan-gen ab, ob es mir denn ent-

weep - ing? And nev - er mark'd their flow? And nev-er mark'd their flow?
gan - gen, dass ich ge-wei-net hab'? dass ich ge-wei - net hab'?

Oh! teardrops, heavy teardrops, What is it chills ye
Ei Thrä-nen, mei-ne Thränen, und seid ihr gar so

thro' That in-to ice ye're turning Like drops of ear-ly dew? And
lau, dass ihr er-starrt zu Ei-se, wie küh-ler Mor-gentau? Und

DIE HIRTEN
(The Shepherds)

Peter Cornelius
Translation by Henry Clough-Leightner

Peter Cornelius

An - - gels sing with ac - cord: "Glo - - ry be to the
En - - gel sin - gen um - her: „Gott im Himmel sei

Lord! And on earth peace and good - will to
Ehr'! Und den Men - - schen hie - nie - - den to sei

mor - tals! On earth be
Frie - den! Den Men schen hie -

good - will to mor - tals!" On-ward the
nie - - den sei Frie - den!" Ei-len die

THE ISLAND

English version by Carl Engel

Sergei Rachmaninoff

LET EACH GALLANT HEART

John Turner

Henry Purcell

thou-sand times more Sweets and de - lights, than your dull,__ your dull__

peace be - fore, than your dull,__ your dull,__ dull__ peace be - fore. Long

tor - ment 'tis sure, We must calm - ly__ en - dure, Be - fore the dear

prize we ob - tain. Yet still the hard toil__ Is part of the cure, And such

plea-sures we find in our pain, That the war - fare of love Yields a thou-sand times more Bliss - ful de - lights Than your dull___ your dull___ peace be - fore, Than your dull, your dull,___ dull___ peace be - fore.

LIKE THE SHADOW

from Time and Truth

George Frideric Handel

Like the sha-dow, life e-ver is fly-ing, All un-no-tic'd so swift the de-lu - - - - sion, so swift the de-lu- -

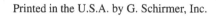

-sion, e - ver is fly - ing,

swift the de - lu - sion! Like the sha - dow, life

e - ver.... is fly - ing, all un - no-tic'd, so swift

the de-lu - -sion.

Fine

Fine

MEMORY

William Blake

John Ireland

Me - mor-y, hi-ther come And tune your

mer-ry notes; And while up-on the wind Your mu-sic

floats,................................. I'll pore up-on the

stream, Where sighing lov-ers dream, ... And fish for

fan-cies as they pass With-in the wa-ter-y glass, ...

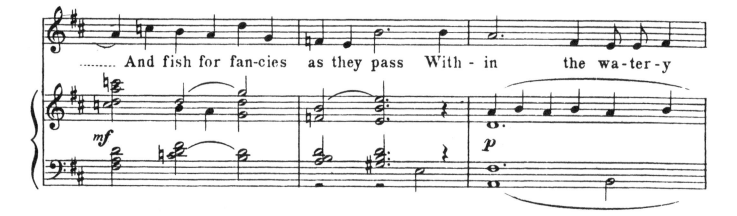

.... And fish for fan-cies as they pass With-in the wa-ter-y

glass. I'll drink of the clear

stream, And hear the lin-net's song, And there I'll lie and

dream The day a - long;........................ And when night comes I'll

go To plac-es fit for woe, Walk-ing a-long the

dark - en'd val-ley, With si - lent Mel-an-chol-y.

DER LINDENBAUM

(The Linden Tree)

from Die Winterreise
by Wilhelm Müller
Translation by
Theodore Baker

Franz Schubert

By the well be-fore the
Am Brun-nen vor dem

door-way There stands a lin-den tree,
To-re, da steht ein Lin-den-baum;

How oft be-neath its
ich träumt' in sei-nem

shad-ow Sweet dreams have come to me; Up-on its bark when mus-ing Fond
Schat-ten so man-chen sü-ssen Traum. Ich schnitt in sei-ne Rin-de so

words of love I made, And joy a-like and sor-row Still
man-ches lie-be Wort; es zog in Freud' und Lei-de zu

drew___ me to its shade.
ihm___ mich im-mer fort.

To -
Ich

62

day, I now must wan - der All thro' the deep-est night; I
musst' auch heu - te wan - dern vor - bei in tie - fer Nacht, da

pass'd it in the dark - ness, I screen'd it from my sight. The
hab' ich noch im Dun - kel die Au - gen zu - ge - macht. Und

branch - es rust-led gen - tly As if they spoke to me: Come
sei - ne Zweige rausch - ten, als rie - fen sie mir zu: komm

here, be-lov'd com - pan - ion, Here peace shall smile on thee.
her zu mir, Ge - sel - le, hier find'st du dei - ne Ruh'!

The cru - - el winds were
Die kal - - ten Win - de

blow - ing So cold - - ly in my
blie - - sen mir grad in's An - ge -

face, My hat was borne be -
sicht, der Hut flog mir vom

hind me, I sped with quick - er
Ko - - pfe, ich wen - - de - te mich

pace.
nicht.

Now man - y leagues I'm far from The dear old lin - den
Nun bin ich man-che Stun - de ent - fernt von je - nem

tree, I ev - er hear it mur - mur "Peace thou wouldst find with
Ort, und im - mer hör' ich's rau - schen: du fän - dest Ru - he

me."   Tho' man - y leagues I'm far___ from   The dear   old lin-den
dort!   Nun bin   ich man-che Stun - de   ent-fernt   von je - nem

tree,   I ev - er hear it mur - mur, "Peace thou___wouldst find with
Ort,   und im - mer hör' ich's rau - schen: du fän - dest Ru - he

me,"   "Peace thou___wouldst find___with   me."
dort,   du fän - dest Ru - he dort!

LORD GOD OF ABRAHAM

from Elijah

Felix Mendelssohn

Draw near, all ye peo-ple, come to me!

Lord God of A-braham, I-saac, and Isra-el; this day let it be known that Thou art God, and I am thy ser-vant! Lord God of A-braham! O shew to all this people that I have done these things according to Thy word! O hear me,

Lord, and an-swer me! O hear me, Lord, and answer me! Lord God of Abraham,

I-saac and Is-ra-el; O hear me, O hear me and an-swer me, and shew this people that

Thou art Lord God, and let their hearts again be turn-ed; O shew this peo-ple that

Thou art Lord God, and let their hearts a-gain be turn-ed, Lord,

and let their hearts, and let their hearts again be turn-ed!

LOVE IS A BABLE

Robert Jones

C. Hubert H. Parry

Printed in the U.S.A. by G. Schirmer, Inc.

can - not tell what.

Love's fair in cra - dle, Foul in fa - ble, 'Tis ei - ther too cold or too

hot; An ar - rant li - ar,___ Fed by de - sire,

It is And yet it is not.

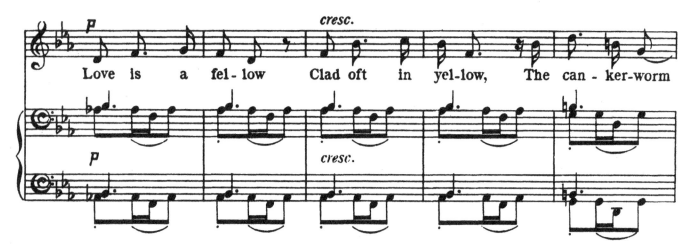

Love is a fel-low Clad oft in yel-low, The can-ker-worm

— of the mind,_____ A pri-vy mis-chief, And such

— a sly thief No man knows which way to find.

Love is_ a_ won-der Thats here_ and yon-der, As com-mon to

one as to moe; A monstrous cheat-er,

Ev' - ry man's debt-or; Hang him and so let him go,

hang_____ him and so let him go.

MATTINATA

English version by Lorraine Noel Finley

Ruggiero Leoncavallo

ro - ra   di bian - co   ve - sti - ta _____   Già l'us - cio dis - chiude al   gran
dawn in   her man - tle   of white - ness _____   Has turned shin - ing eyes_ to   the

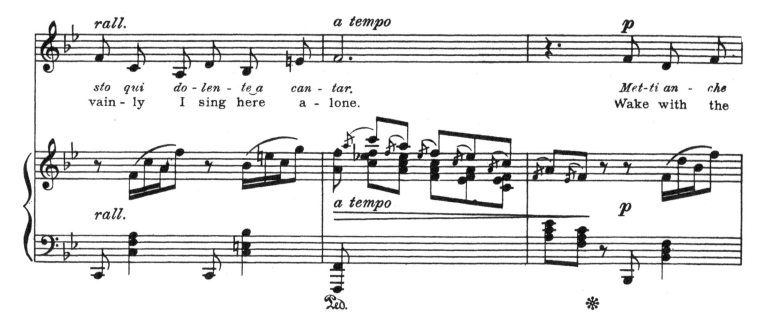

sto qui do - len - te_a can - tar.
vain - ly I sing here a - lone.
Met-ti an - che
Wake with the

tu la___ ve - ste bianca e schiu - di l'u - scio al tuo can-
dawn, ra - diant in glad-ness. O - pen the por - tal; I sing for

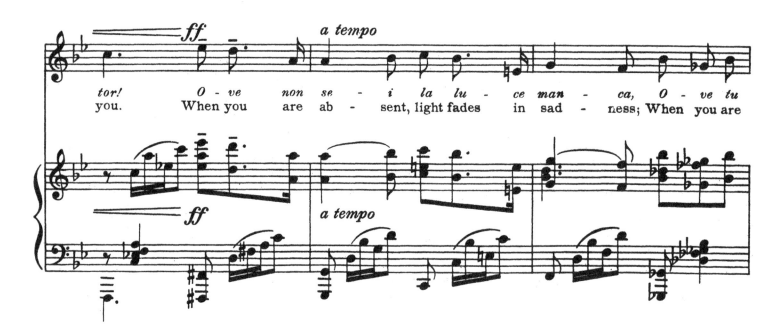

tor! O - ve non se - i la lu - ce man - ca, O - ve tu
you. When you are ab - sent, light fades in sad - ness; When you are

se - i nas - ce l'a - mor!   Met-ti an - che tu   la_ ve - ste
near_ me, love's dream comes true.   Wake with the dawn,   ra - diant in

bianca   e schiu - di l'u - scio al tuo can - tor!   O - ve   non
glad-ness.   O-pen   the por - tal; I sing   for you.   When you   are

se - i la lu - ce man - ca, O - ve tu se - i nas - ce l'a - mor!
ab - sent, light fades in sad - ness; When you are near_me, love's dream comes true.

MORE SWEET IS THAT NAME

from Semele

George Frideric Handel

PLAISIR D'AMOUR

(The Joys of Love)

English version by H. Millard

Giovanni Martini

Plai-sir d'a - mour _____ ne
The joys of love _____ e'er

du - re qu'un mo - ment: _____ cha - grin d'a -
swift - ly do _ de - part, _____ Its sor - rows

mour du - re tou - te la vi - - - e.
bit - ter thro'_ a life - time _____ prove.

J'ai tout quit -
I gave up

té pour l'in - gra - te Syl - vi - - - e; _____
all_ for cru - el Syl - - via's _____ love, _____

cresc.   *f*   *dim.*   *p*

el - - le me quit - te et prend un au - tre _ -
Too soon I find an - oth - er owns her _____

cresc.   *dim.*

"Tant que cet-te eau cou - le - ra dou - ce - ment _____ vers
"Long as this brook - let shall soft - ly on - ward flow, _____ The

ce ruisseau qui bor - de la _ prai - ri - e je t'ai - me -
mead - ow pass - ing on _ its joy - ous way, _____ Thee I _ will

rai," me ré - pé - tait _ Syl - vi - e.
love," ev - er would Syl - via say: _____

L'eau _____ cou - le en - cor, _____ el - le a _ chan - gé _ pour
Still _____ flows the stream, _____ but chang'd is Syl - via

con dolore

tant.— Plai - sir d'a -
now.— The joys of

mour —— ne du - re qu'un mo - ment:— cha - grin d'a -
love —— e'er swift - ly do — de - part,— Its sor - rows

mour du - re tou - te la vi - - e.
bit - ter, bit - ter thro' a life - - time prove.

NATURE'S ADORATION

Ludwig van Beethoven

Andante maestoso.

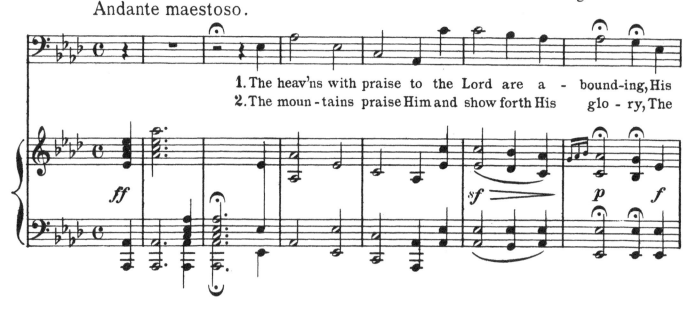

1. The heav'ns with praise to the Lord are a - bound-ing, His
2. The moun - tains praise Him and show forth His glo - ry, The

name to bear a - far they re - joice; The earth, the sea to his
might - y seas His wis - dom de - clare; The hills and vales tell the

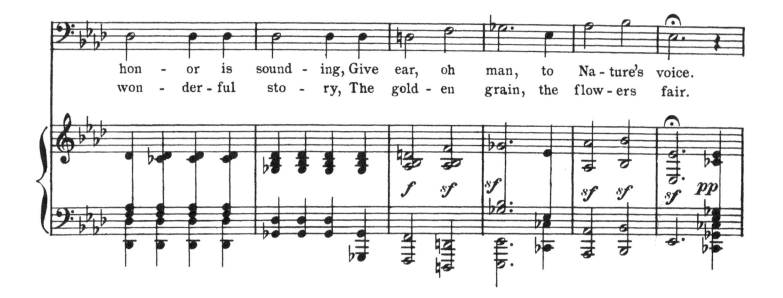

hon - or is sound - ing, Give ear, oh man, to Na - ture's voice.
won - der - ful sto - ry, The gold - en grain, the flow - ers fair.

PIÙ VAGA E VEZZOSETTA

(More Desirable and Pretty Will You Be)

Giovanni Bononcini

va-ga e vez - zo - set - ta Sa - rai se nel tuo co - re Dai

luo-go al - la pie - tà, dai luo-go al - la pie - tà,

Più vaga e vezzosetta sarai
Se nel tuo core dai luogo alla pietà!

Prettier and more graceful you will be
If in your heart you will make a place for sympathy!

Printed in the U.S.A. by G. Schirmer, Inc.

al - la pie - tà!

con anima

p

Più va-ga e vez - zo-set - ta   Sa-

p

(leggiero)

cresc.

rai   se nel tuo co - re   Dai luo - go al - la pie - tà

cresc.

al - - - - la pie - tà;   Più va-ga e vez - zo-

p

set - ta   Sa - rai   se   nel   tuo   co - re   Dai luo-go al - la pie -

tà, _____ al - la pie - tà,   dai luo - go al - la pie -

tà.

Non ve-di, o sem-pli-cet - ta, Che

Non vedi, o semplicetta,
Che scema il tuo rigore
I pregi alla beltà?

Don't you see, you fool,
That your hardness diminishes
The quality of your beauty?

sce-ma il tuo ri - go - re I pre-gi al-la bel-tà, che

sce-ma il tuo ri - go - re i pre-gi al-la bel-tà. Non

ve-di, o sem-pli-cet-ta; che sce-ma il tuo ri - go - re i

pre-gi al-la bel-tà, i pre -

un poco allargando

a tempo

gi al - la bel - tà,   i pre - gi al - la bel - tà.   Più

va - ga e vez - zo - set - ta   Sa - rai se nel tuo co - re   Dai

luo - go al - la pie - tà,   dai luo - go al - la pie - tà,___

___ dai luo - - - - - go al - la pie - tà.   Più

(La var. dal Segno ✛ al ✛ non si trova nell' originale.)

THE POLICEMAN'S SONG

from The Pirates of Penzance

W.S. Gilbert

Arthur Sullivan

When the en-ter-pris-ing burglar's not a - burgling,(not a-burgling.)When the cut-throat is-n't oc-cu-pied in crime,(-pied in crime,) He__ loves to hear the lit-tle brook a-gurgling,(brook a-gurgling,)And lis-ten to the mer-ry vil-lage chime.(village chime.)When the cos-ter's fin-ish'd jump-ing on his

mo-ther,(on his mother,)He loves to lie a-bask-ing in the sun. (in the sun.) Ah, take

one consid-er-a-tion with an-oth-er (with another,)A policeman's lot is not a hap-py one. Ah, When con-

-sta-bu-la-ry du-ty's to be done, to be done, A po-liceman's lot is not a hap-py

one, hap-py one!

DIE POST

(The Post)

from Die Winterreise
by Wilhelm Müller
Translation by Theodore Baker

Franz Schubert

Yes, from the town the post is here,   Where
Nun ja, .die Post kommt aus der Stadt,   wo

once I had_ a love so dear, my   heart! _____
ich ein lie - bes Lieb - chen hatt', mein   Herz! _____

Where once I had_ a love so dear,
wo ich ein lie - bes Lieb - chen hatt',

Oh __ heart, _____ poor__ heart! _____
mein __ Herz, _____ mein __ Herz!

LES ROSES D'ISPAHAN

(The Rose of Ispahan)

Leconte de Lisle
English words by Marion Farquhar

Gabriel Fauré

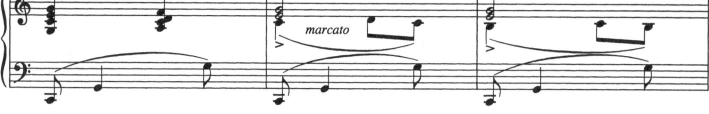

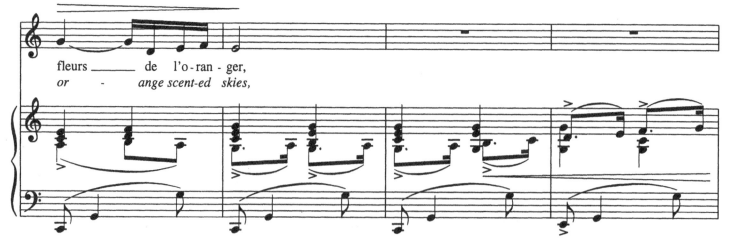

Ont un par - fum moins frais, ont u - ne o-deur moins dou - ce,
Have a per-fume less fresh, have a per-fume less fra - grant,

O blan - che Le - ï - lah! que ton souf - fle lé - ger.
O fair - est Le - i - lah! than thy light - est of sighs.

Ta
Thy

lè - vre est de co - rail, et ton ri - re lé - ger Son - ne
lips are cor - ral red and thy laugh - ter is light As the

ger, Re - vien-ne vers mon cœur d'u-ne ai - le prompte et dou -
frail, Might flut-ter t'ward my heart to ban - ish all my loss -

cresc. poco a poco

ce. Et qu'il par - fu - me en-cor la fleur de l'o-ran - ger,
es, To per - fume a-gain for me the or-ange blos-som pale,

poco rit.   *a tempo*

f

Les ro - ses d'Is-pa-han dans leur gaî - ne de mous -
The rose of Is-pa-han in its sheath - ing of moss -

se!
es!

SALVATION BELONGETH UNTO THE LORD

Maurice Greene

Sal - va - tion be -

long - eth, be - long - eth un - to the Lord. Sal - va - tion be -

long - eth un - to the Lord,_ and thy bless - ing_ is up -

on_ thy_ peo - ple.   Sal - va-tion be-

long-eth,   be - long-eth un -to the Lord,

and thy bless-ing_ is up - on_ thy_ peo - ple,   thy

bless-ing,   thy bless - - ing,   thy bless - -

-ing is up-on— thy peo-ple.   Sal -

va-tion be-long-eth un-to the Lord, and thy bless-ing, thy bless - -

-ing, thy bless-ing is—up-on— thy—peo-ple, thy bless - ing is   up-

on   thy peo-ple, thy bless-ing is up-on— thy peo - ple.

rall.

SI, TRA I CEPPI

(Howsoever they may revile me)

English version by Theodore Baker

George Frideric Handel

Come alla breve

Sì, tra i
How - so -

cep - pi e le ri - tor - te la mia fè ri - splen - de - rà,___
ev - er they may re - vile me, Shall my faith re - splen - dent shine,-

la mia fè ri - splen - de - rà la mia fè, la mia fè ri - splen - de - rà!_____
shall my faith re - splen-dent shine, shall my faith, shall my faith re - splen - dent shine!_____

Sì, tra i
How-so-

cep-pi e le ri-tor-te la mia fè ri-splen-de-rà.
ev-er they may re-vile me, Shall my faith re-splen-dent shine.

Sì, tra i cep-pi e le ri-tor-te la mia fè ri-splen-de-
How-so-ev-er they may re-vile me, Shall my faith re-splen-dent

rà,—
shine,—

la mia fè ri-splen-de-rà,—
shall my faith re-splen-dent shine,—

No, nè pur l'i - stes - sa_ mor - te il mio fo - co e - stin - gue di -
Nor shall death it - self_ com - pel me E'er t'ab - jure the fire di -

rà, _____ no, nè
vine, _____ Nor shall

pur l'i - stes - sa_ mor - te il mio fo - co e - stin - gue - ra.
death it - self_ com - pel me E'er t'ab - jure_ the fire di - vine.

D. C. al fine

SINCE FROM MY DEAR

Henry Purcell

Since from my dear, my dear, _ my dear, _ since from my dear, my

dear, _ my dear, _ my dear, my dear _ As - tre - a's sight I was so

rude — — — — ly torn, My soul _ has ne-ver, ne-ver,

ne-ver, has _ ne-ver, ne-ver, ne-ver known de-light, Un - less it were _ to mourn,_

THE VAGABOND

from Songs of Travel

Robert Louis Stevenson

Ralph Vaughan Williams

Printed in the U.S.A. by G. Schirmer, Inc.

Bed in the bush with stars to see, Bread I dip in the

ri - - ver— There's the life for a man like me,

There's the life for ev - er.

Let the blow fall soon or

late, Let what will be o'er me; Give the face of earth a - round, And the road be

- fore me. Wealth I seek not, hope nor love, Nor a___ friend to

know   me;   All   I   seek,   the heaven a - bove,...........................

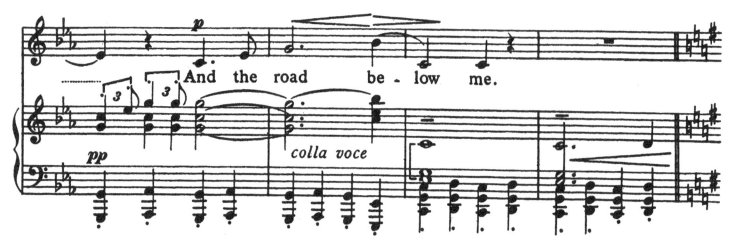

............And   the road   be - low   me.

pp   colla voce

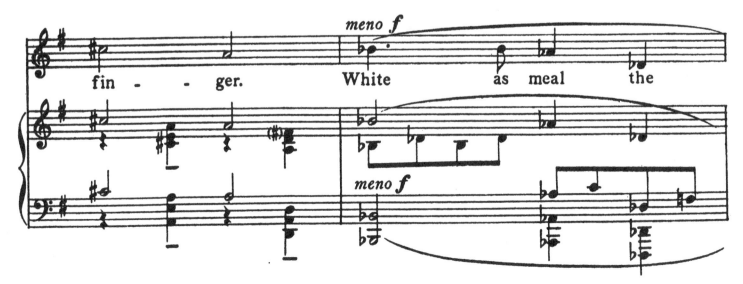

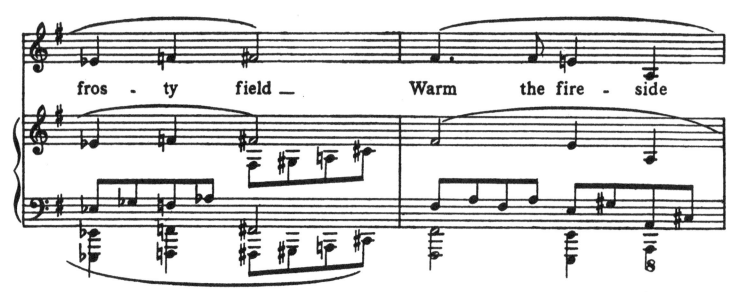

fros - ty field ___ Warm the fire - side

ancora animando.

ha - - - ven ___ Not to

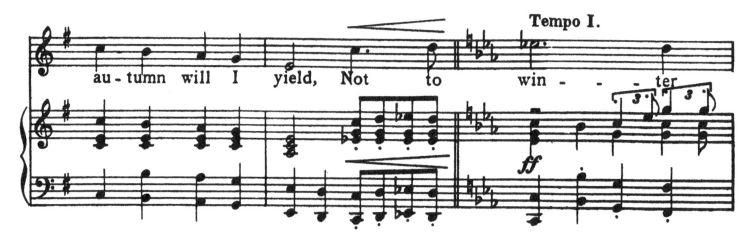

Tempo I.

au - tumn will I yield, Not to win - - ter

e - ven!

dim.

hope nor love, Nor a....... friend to know

me; All I ask, the heaven a - bove,.......................

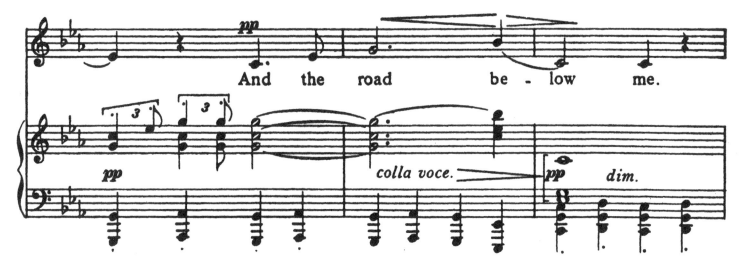

And the road be - low me.

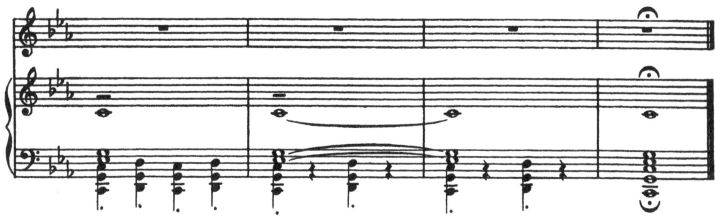

V

DER WANDERER

(The Wanderer)

Schmidt von Lübeck
English version by Willis Wager

Franz Schubert

Ich kom-me vom Ge-bir-ge her,— es dampft das
I come from where the moun-tain soars;— The vale is

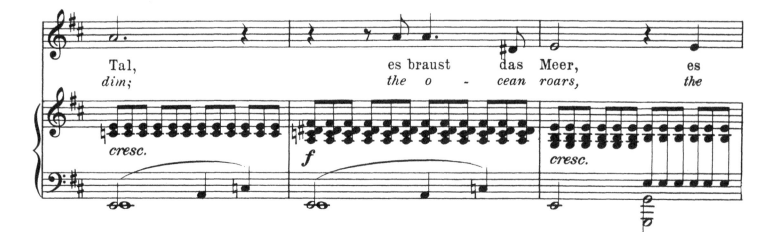

Tal,
dim;

es braust das Meer,
the o - cean roars,

es
the

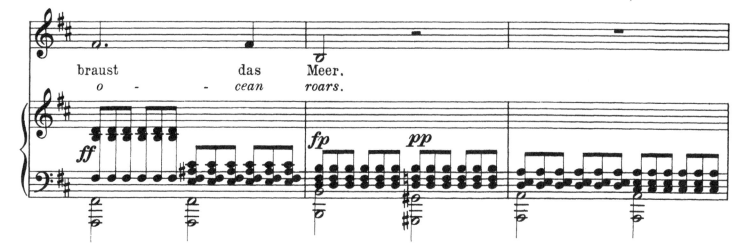

braust das Meer.
o - - cean roars.

Ich wan - dle_ still, bin we - nig froh,
I wan - der_ on, with pain and care;

und im - mer fragt der Seuf - zer, wo? im - mer, wo? Die
My sighs for - ev - er ques - tion "Where?" ev - er "Where?" To

Son - ne dünkt mich hier so__kalt, die Blü - te welk, das Le - ben alt, und
me the sun - light seems too__cold, The flow - ers pale, and life__seems old; Their

was sie re - den, lee - rer Schall,ich bin ein Fremd-ling ü - ber-all.
hol - low phras-es fill__the air, I am a stran-ger ev-'ry-where.

Poco più mosso

Wo bist du, wo bist du, mein ge-lieb - tes Land? ge-
Where art thou, where art thou, dear - est Land, my own, Be-

sucht,___ ge-ahnt,___ und nie _____ ge-
sought,___ di-vined,___ and still _____ un-

Allegro

kannt! Das Land, das Land so hoff-nungs-grün, so
known! The land, the land where hope is sown, where

hoff-nungs-grün, das Land, wo mei-ne Ro-sen blüh'n, wo mei-ne Freun-de
hope is sown, The land where my own rose is grown, Where all my friends their

wan-deln geh'n, wo mei - ne To - ten auf - er-steh'n, das Land, das mei - ne
cus - toms keep, Where my be - lov - ed dead still sleep, The land that speaks my

Tempo I°

Spra - che spricht, o Land, __ wo bist du?
moth - er tongue, O Land, __ where art thou?

Ich wan - dle __ still, bin we - nig froh,
I wan - der __ on, with pain and care;

und im - mer fragt der Seuf - zer, wo? im - mer,
My sighs for - ev - er ques - tion "Where?" ev - er

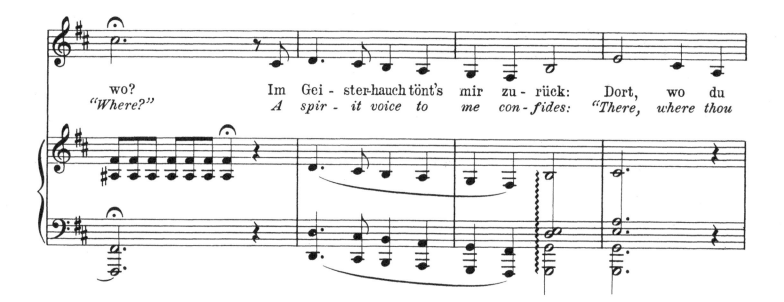

wo? Im Gei - ster-hauch tönt's mir zu - rück: Dort, wo du
"Where?" A spir - it voice to me con - fides: "There, where thou

nicht bist, dort ist das Glück!
art not, all joy a - bides."

WHEN I WAS A LAD I SERVED A TERM

from H.M.S. Pinafore

W.S. Gilbert

Arthur Sullivan

1. When I was a lad I served a term As of - fice boy to an At - tor - ney's firm, I cleaned the win-dows and I

2. As of - fice boy I made such a mark That they gave me the post of a ju - nior clerk. I served the writs with a

swept the floor, And I po-lished up the han-dle of the big front door.
smile so bland, And I co-pied all the let-ters in a big round hand.

I po-lished up that han-dle so care - ful - lee, That
I co - pied all the let-ters in a hand so free, That

now I am the ru-ler of the Queen's Na - vee! I po-lished up that han-dle so
now I am the ru-ler of the Queen's Na - vee! I co-pied all the let-ters in a

care - ful - lee, That now I am the ru - ler of the Queen's Na - vee!
hand so free, That now I am the ru - ler of the Queen's Na - vee!

3. In ser-ving writs I made such a name That an
4. Of le-gal knowledge I acquired such a grip That they

ar - ti-cled clerk I soon be-came; I wore clean col-lars and a
took me in - to the part - ner-ship, And that jun - ior part - ner -

bran' new suit For the pass ex-am-in-a-tion at the In - sti - tute.
-ship I ween Was the on - ly ship that I ev-er had seen.

5. I grew so rich that I was sent By a
6. Now lands-men all, who - ev-er you may be, If you

pock - et borough in-to Par - lia - ment. I al - ways vo - ted at my
want to rise___ to the top of the tree, If your soul is-n't fet-tered to an

par - ty's call, And I nev - er thought of think-ing for my - self at all.
of - fice stool, Be care-ful to be guid-ed by this gold - en rule.

I thought so lit - tle, they re -
Stick close to your desks and

-ward - ed me, By mak-ing me the ru - ler of the Queen's Na - vee. I
nev - er go to sea, And you all may be ru-lers of the Queen's Na - vee. Stick

thought so lit - tle, they re - ward - ed me, By mak-ing me the ru - ler of the
close to your desks and nev-er go to sea, And you

Queen's Na - vee. all — may be ru-lers of the Queen's Na - vee.